4/97

AMERICAN INDIAN FAMILIES

A TRUE BOOK

by

Jay Miller

Children's Press®

A Division of Grolier Publishing

New York London Hong Kong Sydney
Danbury, Connecticut

For help in reading and writing these books, Jay Miller thanks Tamaya, Garrett, Erica, and Aaron.

Reading Consultant
Linda Cornwell
Learning Resource Consultant
Indiana Department of Education

Library of Congress Cataloging-in-Publication Data

Miller, Jay, 1947-
    American Indian families / by Jay Miller.
        p.   cm. — (A true book)
    Includes bibliographical references and index.
    Summary: Introduces the different kinds of family relationships among American Indians and how they varied from one tribe to another.
    ISBN 0-516-20133-6 (lib. bdg.)   ISBN 0-516-26089-8 (pbk.)
    1. Indians of North America—Kinship—Juvenile literature. 2. Indians of North America—Social life and customs—Juvenile literature. 3. Family—United States—Juvenile literature. 4. Social structure—United States—Juvenile literature. [1. Indians of North America—Social life and customs. 2. Family.] I. Title. II. Series.
E98.K48M55 1996
306.85'08997—dc20   96-15164
                                                                                          CIP
                                                                                          AC

Contents

A Navajo family shelters from the sun.

Names Are Important

Almost everyone belongs to a family. Children grow up in families all over the world. Families have always been an important part of American Indian cultures too. Families affected who someone married or how someone grew up, even the words someone used to talk to someone.

American Indians used special terms to talk to or about their relatives. People used these terms because personal names were too sacred to be used in public. These terms could mean more than one person, so that a person had many "mothers" and "fathers."

Among the Delaware, "gahes" meant the woman who gave birth to a child and all of her sisters. And along with the man who would be

called "father" in English,
all of his brothers were also
called "nok."

All of the people older
than a child's parents were
called "grandmother" and

A grandmother carries her granddaughter.

"grandfather." They did the most to raise children, since parents were too busy getting food and making everything needed to survive.

All of the important things in the world were also called by kin terms to show respect. The fire might be called "grandfather." The sun was "father," and the earth "mother" or "grandmother."

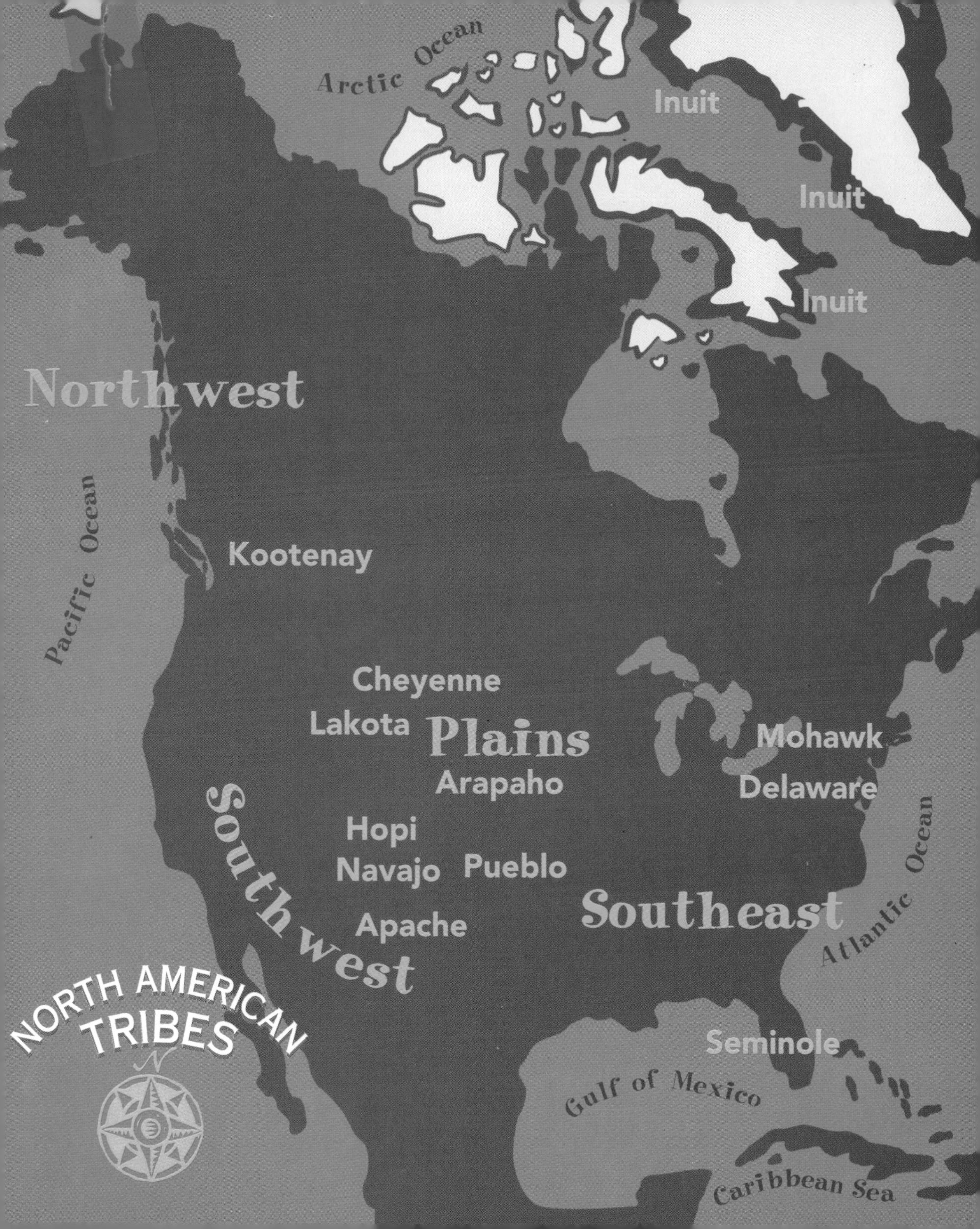
Arctic Ocean
Inuit
Inuit
Inuit
Northwest
Pacific Ocean
Kootenay
Cheyenne
Lakota
Plains
Arapaho
Mohawk
Delaware
Atlantic Ocean
Hopi
Navajo
Pueblo
Southwest
Southeast
Apache
NORTH AMERICAN
TRIBES
N
Seminole
Gulf of Mexico
Caribbean Sea

Families

The smallest group among American Indians was those people who ate together around one fire, what most people would think of as a family.

Married couples and their children made the center of families. Sometimes, an important man had more than one wife. Their children were

Families do many things together—from singing at a picnic to cutting firewood.

raised together. Among a few tribes, when times were hard and people scarce, a woman might have several husbands, but this was rare.

In the West and North of North America, some tribes lived by gathering seeds, nuts, berries, and roots, and by hunting animals. Each family had a tent or house that could be moved so they could go to new sources of food. Families were small—a married couple, their young children, and an older relative or two. Each family belonged to larger groups of kin called bands. A band included everyone on both sides of the

Many Mohawk families lived in a longhouse.

family. Each band shared a
language, customs, and land.
   Elsewhere, farmers and other
tribes with abundant food lived
in large permanent houses with
many fires and families inside.
During feasts and ceremonies
everyone in the house used the
same fire and ate together.

13

Bigger than Families

Families in farming tribes belonged to groups of relatives that were much bigger than families. These were clans, made of all the people who shared one ancestor, traced through mothers or through fathers.

Some tribes put the mother's relatives over the

An Arapaho great-grand-mother with her family—daughter, granddaughter, and great-granddaughter.

father's. In these tribes, fathers were not in charge of their own children. Instead, the oldest brother of the mother helped in raising her children. Why is that? Because the mother, her children, and her brothers were related to each other through the mother and the mother's mother, but the father was not.

The father was related to his own mother and sisters. He taught and trained his own sister's children.

The ancestor of a clan might be a human, but more often it was a spirit who showed special concern for these related fami-

Clans were named after many things. The sun and buffalo were two of

lies. The clan was named after its spirit ancestor. Examples of such names are the Sun, Pine, Flint, Ivy, and Buffalo clans.

A Northwest Coast House was home to people descended from the same ancestor.

Along the Pacific Coast from what is now Canada to California, a special kind of clan exists. It is called the

House, but it is more than just a building. A House is composed of all those people descended from the same spirit or human ancestor.

Other cultures have a similar idea. For example, the Queen of England belongs to the House of Windsor. Each Samurai warrior in Japan belonged to an ancestral house. In the Bible, Jesus belonged to the House of David.

Babies

Much of a family's time was spent raising its children, so that the family would continue.

Families were careful when a baby was coming. Spirits were everywhere, and people needed their help to do anything well, including having a baby. To show the spirits she wished for an easy delivery, a

pregnant woman never stood
in a doorway or blocked a
passage. Other family
members ate carefully so that
the baby would be healthy.

After the baby was born,
mother and newborn remained

apart from everyone else for a certain number of days. Sometimes, a mother and son stayed inside for eight days. A mother and daughter stayed for five days. Sometimes the father did the same to show that he was willing to take on the duties of fatherhood.

If the family was important, the baby was named at the end of the time apart. Children of other families waited until they were older to receive a name from the family or clan.

Often, the father's older sister helped with the naming and made a cradleboard to carry the baby around. Every tribe had its own style of cradleboards to show if the baby was a boy or a girl.

The baby on the left is in a Navajo cradleboard. Babies could sleep in little hammocks when they weren't being carried (below).

Children

Children grew up surrounded by loving relations. More and more, they learned to do what adults did. They learned the ways of plants and animals. They helped cook food. In the Great Lakes, children gathered cranberries because the thin bogs could not support the weight of a grown-up.

By playing with a puppy,
an Inuit girl gets to know a
future sled dog.

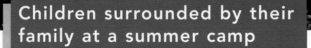

Children surrounded by their family at a summer camp

Important families had par-
ties every time their children
did something for the first
time. The first meat, step, or
spoken word were celebrat-

ed. The Navajo had a party for the first laugh and the Kootenay people for the first whistle. An important milestone came when a boy killed his first animal during a hunt or a girl brought home her first berry or crop.

When boys and girls were old enough, their families sent them to find a spirit who would help them all life long. They had to pray and not eat or drink anything. After a few days

A father helps his son get ready for a pow wow.

a spirit who looked like a person came and told what kind of help it would give. In this way, a person became a carver, potter, singer, or basket maker. Natural ability was not enough. To be a success, someone had to have a spirit helper.

Another big event was coming of age, when boys and girls started to become adults. In ancient times, these changes indicated they were ready for marriage.

Becoming a Woman

When a girl's body starts to change and grow into a woman's, or a boy's body grow into a man's, this is a time of celebration. Soon they will be adults, and will make families of their own. American Indian people have always celebrated this important time, and this tradition continues today.

As part of her ceremony, an Apache girl dances with a friend while men sing the creation story behind her.

She lies
on the
earth and
is molded
like the
earth is
molded, so
that she will have the
power of the earth.
She is blessed with
sacred pollen. Other
rites are performed.
Now she is ready to
become a woman.

Marriage

The elders of both families arranged the marriage because this decision was too important to be left to the youngsters themselves. Yet their wishes were respected. Usually, they didn't have to marry someone they did not like.

A Seminole couple at their wedding in 1930 (left); Navajo family entering a temporary building made just for the wedding (below)

The married couple moved in with one of their families. If the children were traced through the mother, then the newlyweds lived with the family of the bride. If through the father, the couple lived with his family.

Great respect had to be shown to the in-laws. Among the Apache, a son-in-law showed this regard by avoiding his mother-in-law. He could not speak to her or be alone with

Wedding cakes are a new tradition.

her. If he had to tell her some-thing, he spoke to someone or something nearby. A daughter-in-law also avoided her husband's parents, but since she cooked and kept the house for them she did not ignore them totally.

Other kinds of relatives were treated in other ways. Since they were close in age, sisters-in-law and brothers-in-law could be friendly and joke together.

Throughout marriage and life, a person helped anyone in need. They made a contribution to their camp or town. They worked hard. They thought of others. All this upheld family honor.

Growing Old

Everyone hoped to grow old and die surrounded by family. As people got older, they became more religious. They prayed and gave offerings to the spirits. They wanted their family to be well and happy.

Elders prepared for their death. They had fine clothes

An elder

ready to wear for burial. They gave away possessions to their family and friends. The wisest elders had special knowledge. They trained heirs to take their places, and passed on their knowledge to them.

After death, the body was washed and dressed. For several days, everyone gathered to say goodbye to the person who had died. Tribes followed different customs with the body. The bodies of people who

Burial grounds, such as this Hopi one, are holy places.

The Cheyenne used to bury their dead in trees.

belonged to the Cheyenne were once placed in trees. Eventually, the remains were buried.

Chiefs were buried some place that overlooked their people. Doctors were placed away from towns. In death, they were too powerful to keep nearby. Only their relatives visited these lonely graves.

The ghost went on to a land where all of the ancestors of the tribe continued to exist. There, it was welcomed by all its dead relatives.

The living and the dead continued to visit sometimes, since they were still related.

A memorial pow wow honors the dead.

Related to All Things

For American Indians,
relatives were everywhere.
The connectedness of all
things extended beyond
death. Indians knew they were
just one part of everything.
They respected anything older
than themselves and shared
what they had. At the end of

A grandmother helps her grandchild at a pow wow.

prayers, Lakota Sioux sum up all of these beliefs by giving thanks to the entire world of "All my relations."

To Find Out More

Here are some additional resources to help you learn more about American Indian families:

Books

Rendon, Marcie R. **Powwow Summer: A Family Celebrates the Circle of Life.** Lerner Publications, 1996.

Swentzell, Rina. **Children of Clay: A Family of Pueblo Potters.** Lerner Publications, 1992.

Wolfson, Evelyn. **Growing up Indian.** Walker and Co., 1986.

Wood, Ted, with Wanbli Numpa Afraid of Hawk. **A Boy Becomes a Man at Wounded Knee.** Walker and Co., 1995.

Videos

Charles, Tony, director. **I Am Different from My Brother.** Native American Public Broadcasting Consortium, 1981.

Organizations

American Indian Community House, Inc.
404 Lafayette Street
New York, NY
212-598-0100

American Indian Heritage Foundation
6051 Arlington Blvd.
Falls Church, VA 22044
202-463-4267

Online Sites

Aboriginal Youth Network
http://ayn-0.ayn.ca/

This Canadian site is for young people of all cultures.

Index of Native American Resources on the Internet
http://hanksville.phast. umass.edu/misc/ NAresources.html

Start here to find resources on every aspect of American Indian life and culture.

NativeWeb Home Page
http://web.maxwell.syr.edu/ nativeweb/

This is another excellent starting point, and connection to information about indigenous people all over the world.

Important Words

ancestors relatives from long ago

band a group of related families that share a leader and ancestors

cradleboards baby carriers

culture ideas, actions, and habits that children learn as they grow up in a certain group of people

elder a wise older person

house families from the same ancestor sharing a building

ritual an action that is always done in a certain way as part of an important event

spirit invisible beings with power over the natural world

traditions ancient customs and beliefs

Index

Meet the Author

Jay Miller lives in Seattle, visiting nearby reservations, mountains, streams, and the Pacific Ocean. He enjoys eating salmon and pie, hiking in the mountains, and kayaking along the shore as much as he enjoys being a writer, professor, and lecturer. He has taught in colleges in the United States and Canada. He belongs to the Delaware Wolf clan. His family is delightful and very complex. He has also authored *American Indian Games*, *American Indian Festivals*, and *American Indian Foods* for the True Book series.